Kerry Burton-Galley is a York-born writer, artist, and animal rights activist.

She lives with her husband and their Thai rescue dog, nestled between the Moors and the Dales.

The One Before the First

Kerry Burton-Galley

Copyright © 2025 Kerry Burton-Galley

Copyright © 3 Gargoyles Publishing
Cover image and illustrations Copyright © Kerry Burton-Galley
Cover font created with the use of myscriptfont.com
The right of Kerry Burton-Galley to be identified as the author
of this work has been asserted by her in accordance
with section 77 and 78 of the Copyright,
Designs and Patents Act, 1988.
All rights reserved.

No part of this publication may be reproduced or transmitted
or utilized in any form or by any means
(electronic, mechanical, photocopying or otherwise)
without permission in writing from the publisher.

Author photo Copyright © Tom Woollard.

'Courage' by Kyla La Grange
Copyright © Sony Music Entertainment UK Ltd.
All rights reserved.

Every effort has been made to contact the copyright holders
of the original source material included in this book.
Where the attempt has been unsuccessful
the publisher would be pleased to rectify any omission.

ISBN: 978-1-0684629-0-0

This is a work of creative non-fiction.
The events portrayed are to the best of the author's memory.
However, names, places and other details have either been altered or
omitted entirely in order to protect the privacy of the people involved.

'You say I have a heart of gold
and a body that you long to hold
and it kills me.
You say you like my company
you'll spend all my time
but you don't love me…'

Courage
Kyla La Grange

For the heart that carried these words around
long before I could write them down.

Contents
I

The Storyteller.................................. 1
Prey.. 2
Coppergate Magpie......................... 3
Revived.. 4
Recognition..................................... 5
You in the Queue........................... 6
Well, I Mean—You Look Good!......7
Hades.. 8
Proximity...10
Lovely, Dark and Deep.................. 11
Sinister.. 12
Still Pool..14
Ghosts... 15
Overlooked..................................... 16
Kelly.. 17
A Few Weeks.................................. 18
Turned Back...................................19
Spinning... 20
Bus Ticket....................................... 21
To Die and Live, To Live and Die.. 22
Wainwright..................................... 23
Sweat... 24
Tray of Tea...................................... 25
The Surgeon................................... 26
Separated.. 27
Caught... 28
The Realisation...............................29
Virgin.. 30
Hell Breaking Loose...................... 31
Your Laugh.....................................32
Future Enemies..............................33
Escorted to Boyes.......................... 34
Cast.. 35
Good Company.............................. 36
For My Mum.................................. 37
Girl...38
Clifford's Tower............................. 39
Clever Ghoul.................................. 40
Transparent.................................... 41
I Picked You................................... 42

Temple..43
Under the Skin...............................44
Nerdy Things................................. 45
Sunshine Again.............................. 47
Your Children................................ 48
Emotional Wishlist........................ 49
Guilt Makes it Better..........50
Lilith..51
The Gallery..................................... 53
Tulips.. 54
Lounger...55
Bitter Lemonade............................56
That Long?......................................57
Tearoom Tongue............................58
Kellbalk Lane................................. 59
Lost..60
Sweetheart...................................... 61
The Answer.....................................62
Hesitate... 63
Research... 64
Do You Have Orgasms?....65
Big Predator................................... 66
Slow Burner.................................... 67
Wilder the Wind............................ 68
Dracula Was Here......................... 69
Whitby.. 70
Female Insects................................71
Courteous Carnivore...........72
July Seventeenth............................73
The Bookshop................................ 75
Bitten... 76
Slowly Melting Icebergs..... 77

II

Wasted..78
Awkward..79
Status..80
One or Two Others............................81
Leaflet Girl...82
Ugly...83
Late..84
Barcelona..85
The Right..86
Different Worlds................................87
Provocative Statement.......................88
Unchanged...89
The Hug..90
No More..92
McCain? Oven Chips........................93
Flat 6...94
Shelf..95
The Last Time I Saw You.................96
For Now..97
Heavy Stone.......................................98
Absence...99
Possible...100
Break Up...101
21/58..102
Reminders...103
Words..104
Almosts..105
Reliance...106
The Market Square..........................108
Still..110
The Plea...111
York...112
X O'Clock...114
October..115
Morality Jar......................................117
Memories Invade the Night............118
Thud..119
Ad Hominem....................................120
Everybody But Me...........................121
Maggoty Work..................................122
Rare...123
Impulse..125
Fool...126

Six-Stone-Thirteen...........................127
The Wolf Spider and I.....................128
Strangers...130
The Shoebox.....................................131
Ashes...132
Chess...133
Three Videos....................................134
Your Name..135
Summertime.....................................136
The Pretend Partaker........................137
Pretty Dresses...................................138
Brown Quilted Coats........................139
Top Hats and Canes..........................140
September...141
Relentless...142
Bullseye..143
Esteem..144
Flesh Covered Skeleton...................145
Red Raggedy Jumper.......................146
I'm Sorry...147
The One..148

III

The First..151
Inside Number 9...............................153

I

The Storyteller

The slick, aging crow of night
carried his beloved cane
with devilish delight.
The moon was bright
to conjure fright
as he came to a stop,
turned, and whispered—
"And so, it was midnight…"

Prey

Back then, I relied—heavily—on Google Maps
just to help me find my fearful little way
from Exhibition Square
to Coppergate.

Back then, I fretted into the early hours,
not about meeting an unknown male with
thirty years, five stone, and ten inches on me—
no.

But about being at the right café.

Back then, I felt physically sick
at the thought of ordering a cup of tea,
not knowing whether to sit,
or to stand and pay.

I had visions of myself
dropping the tray.

Back then, I was so terrified
I'd get on the wrong number bus,
end up far from home,
all alone—

and yet somehow,
you still felt like the prey.

Coppergate Magpie

Are you here to soothe me,
a symbol of reassurance?

Are you telling me this is fate—
that this is where life begins?

That I'll be happy?
Or are you a warning
of the sorrow to come—
a dark little nod
toward becoming crushed
and numb?

Coppergate magpie,
something in me knows
it's both.

And God help me,
my feathered friend,
I'm helpless
to stop myself.

Revived

It was like being revived from the dead,
like all my chronically numbed neurons
finally sparked to life inside my head.

Warmth like honey trickled through my brain,
and within just a second, that feeling
had oozed through every vein.

A decade of pent-up misery and dread
was drawn from my heaving lungs
that'd weighed me down like lead.

The constricting grip around my heart
slackened as you drew ever closer—
your very being was a tranquilizing dart.

You were still an unknown,
but some kind of primal recognition
told me your soul held part of my own.

Recognition

I mouthed your name.
Too shy to speak it out loud.

You looked right through me, eyes unfixed,
my presence folding into the mix
of tables, mugs, and lunchtime chatter.
And I shrank, feeling like I'd shatter.

Then—
your face lit like a match.

And I knew then
you'd seen me

the way I saw you.

You in the Queue

I kept my eyes on the page—
or tried to.

'The Pianist'
page twenty-two.

But then I glanced at you in the queue.

Again.
And again.
I mean—

there are men.
And then there's you.

Well, I Mean—You Look Good!

You asked if I was alright now
after I told you I'd been ill.
And then it escaped you—
"Well, I mean—you look good!"

"Thank you,"
I said—
bowing my head,
quiet, polite,
inwardly set alight.

When I looked up,
you were searching my face
for a flicker,
a flush.

Don't get me wrong,
I felt the rush,
but I'd be damned
to present as anything
but strong.

It was
quite the performance,
for a girl with no confidence.

Hades

It was as though
I myself
had whittled his bones,
as if
with my own
bare hands
I had
moulded
every sinew.

His pale
freckled flesh
I could have spun,
then drawn
each line
and,
into each follicle,
sewn a silver
or copper curl.

Each
of his
ivory teeth
I could have carved,
polished,
and placed precisely.

His fingers,
his
padded palms,
I might have stuffed
with the warmest
of fibres.

But
I suspect
I would have had to collect
crystalline sands
from the deepest,
bleakest
pools of Hades
to blow the glass needed
for such sombre eyes
as those.

Proximity

Had I moved
just one inch,
our knees
would have touched.

I contemplated it:
I'd always hated it—
being this close
to anyone.

But not to you.

Lovely, Dark and Deep

You sat
reciting Frost,
eyes fixed,
unblinking,
as though the lines
were still unfolding.

Afterwards,
you said the horse
couldn't see the beauty
a man sees.

And I thought—
no, but I can.

It is you—
not the woods—
who is lovely,
dark,
and deep.

Sinister

There's just something
so alluringly
sinister...

You know,
you remind me
of Hannibal Lecter.

And it's funny—
my friend,
she calls me "Kerrice".

I think
not just because,
like Clarice,

I'm a
sullen,
highly principled loner,

obsessed
with what makes
a murderer,

but because I'm
drawn to men who are
uncommonly courteous

as well as being
oh so dreadfully
dangerous.

So,
you see,

I'm not intimidated.

If anything,
it makes me
all the more fixated.

Still Pool

You once described me
as a still pool—
reflective,
composed,
not much going on
at the surface.

But underneath,
churning depths.

Perhaps a siren
luring men
to untimely deaths.

Question is:
how much do you like
to swim?

Ghosts

You asked me to find it
'Ghosts' by Mortimer—you'd forgotten the title
but delivered it in that trance-like way again,
as I, in private awe, wrote it down in pen.

Later, finding it was vital.
I discovered you'd misquoted one line.

The original wording was just fine,
but your version was profound and divine.

Overlooked

There was a small cluster
of shining, silver hairs
you'd missed.

It made me think
you weren't married.
Or if you were,
I guessed you were often
dismissed.

Kelly

You called me Kelly.
I corrected you.
But I couldn't be annoyed—
not when you squeezed your eyes shut
in embarrassment,
and leant your head forwards,
towards my chest.

My tart of a heart
flung itself
against my ribs.

Upon reflex,
I stopped breathing,
as if to restrain it.

If I had been braver,
less polite,
less me—
I'd have cradled your face,
or run the backs of my fingers
down your cheek,
like an archaeologist
who'd uncovered
the skull of a lifetime
that she'd been delicately unearthing
all week.

A Few Weeks

When I told you
how long it had taken,
you repeated it,
fascinated,
under your breath.

It was a level
of appreciation
I hadn't
quite expected.

What you didn't know
was I'd burnt
my two drawing fingers—
and still kept going
knowing

it was a warning.

Turned Back

You stopped at the door,
turned back,
and held the envelope
to your chest.

Your hand rested over it—
tenderly,
like it was something sacred.

But that weight of sadness
returned to your face,
as if you were sad
to be leaving this place.

"You're welcome,"
I said—
too flat,
too quiet,
even for me.

I reached for my bag,
wrapped my scarf
around my neck.

When I looked up—
you were gone.

Spinning

A deep, shaking breath.
After he left.
All the sounds came back—
the clatter, the chatter,
the cutlery.
The world was loud.
Too loud.
Cold,
but new.
I felt warm.
Briefly.
Content.
Then—
with every passing second,
increasingly
empty.
The businesspeople
to my right
were eyeing me funny.
Then the waitress came
to clear his mug.
She glanced at me,
not quite smiling.
I said, "Thank you."
Then quickly left.
What was I missing?
Mind the traffic.
Concentrate.

I forgot something—
something feels missing—
the soulmate.

Bus Ticket

I still have my bus ticket
from the day we met.
It's see-through thin
and it's faded quite a bit,
but of all the things I've kept,
this is still my favourite.

I think the bus driver
thought I was a right twit,
but I just couldn't bear
to part with it.
I realised, with a smile,
when I went to go sit—
in just one hour with you,
I'd already grown in spirit.

To Die and Live, To Live and Die

Last month, I sat
desolate, at my mum's bedside,
I was so overcome
with bitterness and fear
that I think I died on the inside;
it felt like life was over
but I couldn't shed another tear.

Last week, I sat
euphoric, in your company,
oh, what it was to feel so content—
and to think I'd been suicidal
less than a month before!
The instant I saw you,
it was like a spiritual revival.

But last night, I sat
cold, in my single bed,
listening to *'One Day'*
by Kodaline,
sobbing silently into my palm
as I came to realise
you'd never be mine.

Wainwright

You said you'd thought of me
while looking at Wainwright's drawing—
my memory, gently gnawing.
I blinked—
breath caught
that you'd so much as
spared me a thought.

Sweat

You ran across town
so I wasn't kept waiting.
Your forehead shone
with effort and care.

It was that.
The run.
The sweat.

For me.

Tray of Tea

You offered me a bun.
Twice.

I said no.
Twice.

Your shoulders dropped
in playful disappointment.

So you brought a whole tray of tea—
but didn't pour a single cup.
You just sat,
hands in the air—
a man swearing
he came in peace.

The gesture was
so chivalrous
and just so
beautifully,
perfectly
ridiculous.

The Surgeon

You gifted me an art print,
told me some said they saw
healing,
hard work,
hope.

But others saw
something colder—
a contained madness,
pain.

You asked which I saw.

Naturally,
you'd seen
the same.

Separated

"...Been married thirty years," you said.

Fist in the heart.
Fist in the stomach.

I looked away.
Eyes down the side of the table.
Needed a minute.

"But we're separated now..."

A hand gesture—firm,
as if pushing your whole life
to one side.

I wanted to believe you.
God, I wanted it.
But my head split open
with suspicion.

You told me
you're not that kind of man—
the kind who runs to someone else.
You said it with weight,
like it's important
that I know.

I want to believe in you.
So badly.

Maybe you were meant for me—
if only for this moment.
I'm an expert at stretching those
to an eternity.

Caught

For reasons beyond me,
and without intent,
my eyes flickered
to your crotch.
Once.
Twice.
And both times
you caught me.
It was less than a second—
but long enough.
Your stare afterwards
was

penetrative.

The Realisation

You said
your thing was to be wanted—
not paid for,
not pitied,
simply fancied.

And I,
gesturing toward you, said:
"Well, why wouldn't they?"

Your face—
when you realised
I'd nearly given it away.

Virgin

You asked if I had a boyfriend.
Abruptly,

like you didn't want me to think.
But I'd rehearsed the answer
for weeks.

"No," I said,
"I haven't had one."

You blinked.

"Since...?"
"Eleven."

And the honesty
hit like cold water.

You stared—
at my shoulders,
my hair,
all the places where other men
had never been
permitted.

Hell Breaking Loose

"So you've never been in love?" you ask.
Bright.
Like it's charming.
Like you're looking forward
to the destruction of me.

I almost say it.

I'm in love now.

With you.
Of course with you.

Instead, I shake my head
with a flat, sad smile.

"I bet you don't believe in it," you grin knowingly.
"That'll be when all hell breaks loose."

I laugh a little too quickly,
and hide behind my hands—

a prison of fingers.

Your Laugh

It was different
to what I'd imagined.

Like a boy's first nervous titter
at a Page Three,

and an old man's
last one—
hollow with memory.

Future Enemies

Even now, I can go back to that precise moment—
you and I were sat beside one another in Caffè Nero,
those glazed blue eyes were boring into mine,
and mine couldn't get enough of the challenge.

We didn't break eye contact, not even for a second.
Both of us were smiling, then, edging on laughter,
when thoughts I'd buried from the start, piped up:

One day, probably not so many months from now,
he'll pin all this on me, and make me his enemy.

And—rightly or wrongly—
I still gazed longingly.

Escorted to Boyes

You touched my arm,
and I didn't even feel it
through the wool.
Too quick.
Too light.
Too unexpected.
But the shock of it
stayed in my chest
for hours.
I kept rewinding the moment
just to try
and feel it again—
properly.

Cast

It wasn't just the touch—
it was the shape.
The fit.
Your warmth
to my cold.
Like your hand
was cast
for mine.

Good company

You told the waiter at Goji:
"Food was good.
Company was better."

And though I dismissed you
as a charmer—a jester,
it meant more to me
than I could measure.

For My Mum

You remembered the wool.
The mugs.
The pain.

You didn't fix anything.
You couldn't.
But you listened.

And that's all I'd ever wanted
from anyone.

Girl

The man at Clifford's Tower
thought I was under sixteen.
You laughed, and I did glower,
but there was something
titillating
in both our glances after.

Clifford's Tower

You touched my lower back
at the top of the tower—
a place built for war.

You told me someone had jumped
once.

I closed my eyes
and leaned into you,
like a momentary ledge.

Clever Ghoul

We were just mooching about
in the bowels of the Castle Museum,
eyeing some ancient torture
and captivity devices used
back when York was still Eboracum,

when you stood and watched
my predicted morbid enthusiasm.
You said it wasn't your idea of pleasure,
but it might be something
you'd attempt to overcome—

if I found it fun.

And then you went and said,
"I think... you have a deep-rooted desire
to control the cruel."

And I was taken aback.
You really are one
remarkably clever ghoul.

Transparent

I'd drowned in my own tears
long before I met you.
And maybe it's because
you'd spent so many years
in the company of ghosts,
but after a lifetime of feeling
completely invisible
to suddenly become
wholly visible,
whilst also remaining
entirely transparent—
felt like a bloody miracle.

I Picked You

I told you—
if you weren't married,
I'd pick you.

But then, you knew
I already had.
And you were glad.

You said,
"If I were thirty years younger…"
You didn't finish.

You didn't have to.
That sentence still finishes itself
in my head
every day.

Temple

You squeezed me goodbye,
kissed me
on the left side of my head—
just
four seconds of tenderness,
of devastating sincerity,
pressed softly
into the temple
of a girl
who would feel it
for the rest of her life.

Under The Skin

You gave me a programme.
It was still warm
from your breast pocket.
I couldn't read the synopsis—
not at first.
I was thinking of your form,
absorbing its heat
like Diazepam.

Nerdy Things

"Here's a nerdy fact for you..."
You're ahead of me,
pointing at the arrow shutters
above the railings.
I can't see them
until I step up beside you,
shoulder to shoulder,
playing at closeness
like we've done all day.

Then—
you shift,
just slightly behind.
Your chin hovers
above my left shoulder,
your voice warm in my ear,
spilling facts.

You say they're rare—
one of the few left
in England.
But it's your voice
I'm studying,
not the walls.

I almost did it.
Turned.
Closed the gap.
Let the moment swallow us whole.
But you step back,
like you heard my thoughts.
Teasing, like you always do.

"...So, yeah. Something nerdy."
And just like that,
you've walked away.

I stand there,
still holding the iron rail,
heat rushing
where your voice had been.
"I like nerdy things," I say.
"I know you do," you smirk.
"I like you, don't I?" I quip.
"*Do you*, though?"

You're walking backwards.
"See... I think if anyone's going to leave this,
it'll be you."
This.
What it is, you never say.
But I do know
I won't be the one to stray.

Sunshine Again

You came walking,
slow and sure,
hands stuffed in pockets,
grin so pure.

Sunlight behind you,
I had to squint—
your white shirt bright,
your smile a hint.

"You brought the sunshine,"
you said.

No. The sun's definitely,
definitely
not mine.

Your Children

You said they were the best thing
that ever happened to you.
And for a second,
I wished
you would say that—
just once—
about me.

Emotional Wish List

First you started with my list of places to go and see,
saying whether it was a trip to the Castle Museum
or an orbit of the moon, you knew I'd be good company.

You said, "When y' get braver, I'll tek y' t' Whitby."
that was us—me: forthright, yet pessimistic and wary;
you: streetwise and well-travelled, but afraid, emotionally.

Or so you said, but you soon opened up to me.
You said I was different, though I took it all to be flattery,
letting you know, from the get-go, I wouldn't fool easily.

But this emotional list you requested from me,
you were asking for it before we'd even kissed.
At the time, I think I smiled, coquettishly and sceptically,

at your apparent preoccupation with the Kings' Screen,
musing about how a part of my life was missing: physicality.
I gave you no list, but spoke of transcendence, tranquillity -

to which you said, "This man you speak of,
sounds as if he's got a lot t' live up to, doesn't he?"
and I said, "Not really..."

thinking, *this man I speak of: he stands before me.*
You're the only one, as you know—all too clearly,
for you've set about ticking off those wishes already.

Guilt Makes It Better

"They say Christians have better sex,"
you murmur, out of nowhere.

"Oh?"
I laugh.

I'm not uncomfortable—
I picture you.
Always you.

"How's that, then?" I ask.

"Because they feel guilt about it."

I rise on my toes
whisper near your neck:

"Except,
you're not religious."

A pause.

You stand still, eyes closed,
grinning.

"I was raised Catholic."

Lilith

I point to three carved figures.
"That's Eve being the temptress—" you say,
"and that's Adam resisting:
'No, no, no,
I can't. I can't do it.'"

I laugh,
but not kindly.

"As if any man
has ever said
'No, no, I can't'"

I lower my voice
into yours—
mocking,
inviting.

"Some do."
you murmur.

I tell you about Lilith—
the one who came first,
before Eve,
before ribs and submission.

The one who refused
to kneel.
Who left Eden
without permission.

She visits men
in their sleep,
rakes her nails

down their torsos,
and leaves them
aching.

The Gallery

You stood over my shoulder,
so close
I could feel your breath
on my ear.

If I had turned
just slightly—
we'd have been art
ourselves.

Tulips

You told me once
about a woman so enamoured,
she brought you tulips—
red ones. The colour of romance.

She was all flustered,
hopeful for a chance.

Well, I'm not bringing flowers.
But you can have
my two lips.

Lounger

Do you have to sprawl out like that?
You're making it so damned hard
not to crawl over and get onto your lap.

And I know you're perfectly aware
of the energy you're putting out there
leant back like you are in that chair,

with those three undone shirt buttons.
You're trying to ignite and provoke me.
Well, congrats – I'm practically molten.

And the way you're gazing at me now
suggests you're quite enjoying
raising more than a few eyebrows.

Seriously: don't tempt me.

Bitter Lemonade

You always ordered
bitter lemonade—
pulled a face,
then sipped it anyway.
I watched, amused.
And quietly thought:
Good thing for me
you like bitter things.

That Long?

You asked when you'd see me again.

A week, likely two.

To which you responded:
"That long?"

Your eyebrows pleaded then.

Tearoom Tongue

I can't remember exactly where we were—
it was some little tearoom, a café,
somewhere near Hovingham, anyway.

But I remember joking about fat fetishes,
whilst subtly admiring your upper-arm freckles.
And I remember the effect it had on my genitals

to see the tip of your tongue just lightly brush
the rim of that big, white coffee cup.
Can a person really be envious of crockery?

Apparently, yup.

Kellbalk Lane

The first kiss—
awkward.
Near my house.

I gave you my cheek
like a coward.

But I replayed it later,
in bed,
rearranging the angle
in my head
so it had landed
where it should have.

Lost

Parked beside a rusted old gate,
you blamed me for getting lost;
for your inability to concentrate.

Last week, I'd stepped off the bus
two stops too early—
in a similar state.

You traced a route
on your trusty AA map,
laid it across your lap
like a Venus fly trap.

You thought it a clever move,
but I'm not some little fly
you can charm or entrap.

I resisted the fatal urge
to say, *what the heck*—
to reach across
and grip the curls
at the back of your neck,
and make out
to the sound
of the softly trickling beck.

Sweetheart

It was a small word.
But my whole body
stilled—
as if some part of me
had been named
for the first time.

The Answer

You called me
a very pretty girl—
full of life,
love,
and desire.

Said you weren't sure
what I wanted from you,
but all was good.

Well, there's no flattery
to which I more aspire.

Don't you know the answer?

You should.

It's you.

You're all I've wanted
since girlhood.

Hesitate

Could it really be feasible?
It just seems so inconceivable.
Men don't go six months without sex—
all those I know would complain
make out they've got ball pain.

So to believe you're playing fair,
that you're not putting it elsewhere,
is just so difficult to accept.

Nestled between your thighs
is a bulge I can't help but visualise.

I want you more than anything—
I just need it to mean something.

Our situations are so complex.
And I know the longer I hesitate,
I'll likely as not

leave it too late.

Research

I approached it like a thesis—
with INTJ precision.

You
are my decision.

Late-night tabs open,
going incognito,
looking at diagrams, tips—
well, I can grind my hips
like no one's business,
and my lack of gag reflex
is sure to impress.

Thing is—I know
that I'll be fire
after so many years
of pent-up desire.

I have no fears.

I just want to ensure
I reduce you to tears.

Do You Have Orgasms?

You were going to ask something,
and I knew what.

You wimped out.
But I pushed.

And when you finally asked
if I had orgasms,

I laughed—
but inside,
I quivered

with how close we were
to you finding out.

Big Predator

Last time I saw you—
just after you barked at a dog statue—
I asked what kind of animal I'd be.

You first said, "A bird of prey."
Wrong, but close.
I took it as a compliment, anyway.

Now you're calling yourself a tiger.
Now saying I'm "like a... like a..."
Go on.
Like a what, exactly?

You go ahead,
big, exotic predator -
compare me to a rabbit, a doe.

I'm a magpie—
sharper,
shrewder.

Don't mistake your size
for power.

Slow Burner

You weren't used
to such a slow pace.
I told you I was different—
and you smiled with affection,
calling me a slow burner.

But I saw it—
the flicker of frustration
beneath the warmth.
The quiet flare
of impatience.

You thought me old-fashioned—
a Victorian candlestick.

But when the power cuts,
and there's nothing artificial to flick,
you don't reach for the strobe—
but a deep wick.

Wilder the Wind

We wandered through Nunnington,
coats brushing like thoughts we didn't say.
The sky was heavy and grey—
undecided, just like you.

We found a bench
between a graveyard and a playground—
each of us closer in time
to one than the other.

You spoke of us making love,
but feared you'd fall short of the part—
still vowed to be my friend for life
if I could bear a lesser heart.

I wanted that—
but also you.

The deeper we talked,
the wilder the wind—
like God was listening in,
telling us we'd already sinned.

Dracula Was Here

We were walking through
the Whitby Abbey Museum
when you stopped to read a sign:

'He was never actually here–
Dracula...'

You scoffed–
muttered,
"That's what you think."

Like you knew better.
Like you'd seen him leave.

And I didn't think it was possible,
but you became
even more spectacular.

Whitby

You said
the best part of today
was our hug.

After I'd just said mine
was the fog.

[Lie.]

Female Insects

You're so fixated on the female,
it teeters on being vengeful—
like we all, collectively,
set you up to fail.

Most specifically,
you liked lady insects—
the kind that eat their lovers
after sex.

You said it
with such reverence,

almost
as if you hoped to be next.

Courteous Carnivore

Goji. El Piano.
You knew all the veggie places to go.
It never dented your ego.

You were otherwise so macho—
yet not too proud
to eat mushroom burgers
in a vegan crowd.

And you dressed for the occasion—
your crisp blue shirt, a light persuasion.
I know it was all part of a larger equation,
and always met with my evasion.

But you were such a courteous carnivore—
never made it feel like a bore, a chore.

And in truth
that still leaves me
a little sore.

July Seventeenth

I've never again worn
my denim, daisy dress.
Still, I keep it—
nonetheless.

We took our time
through Coffee Yard.
I was learning how summer feels
in new, uncertain heels.

Titivillus watched us
from his stone arch—
silent and sly,
he caught my eye.

'*Fix You*' drifted up
from the secret garden below,
like York was onto something
we were yet to know.

You joked
about dying mid-blow—
a stroke, no less—
me later insisting
I had nothing to confess.

A ladybird idled
across your bedroom window,
as I placed my hand
on your chest.
It beat so fast, even at rest.

You said you weren't nervous—
just *alive*.

You said you'd never just
laid with someone.

And I—
I didn't want to
be just someone.

You teased me
about a partition pillow.
But then your fingers
gripped my hip—
your mouth met mine,
insistent, but slow.

I remember it well—
how your tongue scraped
beneath my two front teeth—
on July Seventeenth.

The Bookshop

You went into Waterstones
for a poetry book
you couldn't find.

Typed into the air
to mimic the search.
Said you'd look online.

You said it like a joke.
But I could see
you were still a man
who needed poems.

Bitten

You scratched at your arm,
said you'd been bit—
but you didn't mind it.
In fact,
you quite liked it.

And I was quick to say
I'd be sure
to remember it.

Slowly Melting Icebergs

We were two icebergs,
melting slowly—
and with every interaction
came a new thaw.

And though there was less of me
each time,
I'd have kept coming back
until I was no more.

II

Wasted

You said I was wasted on you—
that I deserved marriage,
children,
a lad my own age;
that I'd make a fierce,
wonderful mother.

I told you
that wasn't what I wanted.

But you didn't hear it.
You never did.

I don't want a little boy,
and I don't want a kid.

It's the definition of rage:
you think it a kindness
as you sentence me
to life in a cage.

Awkward

You sat eating an apple
on the corner near the chemist,
shirt unbuttoned just enough.

You'd have kissed me,
I think.

But I gave you
a stiff, awkward hug instead.

Problem was,
my love for you always felt safer
inside my head.

Status

You were so adamant
that women only want men
for their status.

Told me you were a millionaire,
then looked bemused
when I didn't care.

Said you'd owned a sports car—
and still, it didn't click
when I called you
a pretentious dick.

I was the gerontophile,
enthralled by your eyes,
your posture, your smile.

The sapiosexual
who fell for your mind—
the mournful intellectual,
a touch misaligned.

And I wished you'd see
there are superficial women…
and then there's me.

One or Two Others

You asked—
offhand, (but really planned)—
if one or two others
would have mattered.

Yes.
Yes, they would.
That's the part
you never understood.

Leaflet Girl

You just lied to him, and so casually—
whilst I stood there feeling guilty.

I don't know if you did it for me,
or just to spare yourself my fee.

You passed me off as a leaflet girl,
and it suddenly occurred to me:
you'd said that exact thing to me
about Sylvie.

Ugly

You looked out the window,
eyes watching the street below.

"Most people are ugly."

Just that.
Stated as a fact.

And I didn't disagree.
I seldom do.
I've thought it, too.

Still—
the comment
made me look
a little more closely
at you.

Late

You're twenty minutes late.
No sweat.
No regret.

I sat on the Minster steps,
where once you shone
under the sun—
today, there's none.

Just autumn's chill,
and shadows stretching
as time seems to stand still.

The bells didn't toll.
Town's silence slinks
into my soul.

And now I know,
as sure as the cold—
the novelty's gotten old.

Barcelona

Well, his hands—they landed
on my tense and tender shoulders
like two blunt cleavers.

His palms weighed so heavily,
with his gentle, reassuring shake
unwittingly shaking my whole girlish body.

I realised, from thumb to little finger,
his bones were thicker and wider
than the girth and breadth of my collarbones.

His unused, but evident masculinity—
somehow a relaxant to every aching muscle,
goodbye, my usual bullish ferocity.

My weary body pledged to do anything he bid,
as my eyes rolled up, back into their lids—
but then my innards clenched, and I resisted.

I'd swayed back on my feet, him behind me,
his solid, thudding chest promising safety—
but as he stooped to my left ear and whispered, "Boo."

I just knew—
she'd had you.

The Right

I sat in Theatre Royal,
hands clasped tight
between my thighs,
as if to keep my entrails
from slipping out—
tears smarting in my eyes.

My sternum buckled,
ribs folding inward
like a cowering spider,
and you—so flip,
telling me you'd rowed the whole trip.

That's the preference—strife?
Your ever-loving wife.

How unfathomably cerebral,
to remark I'd have loved the cathedral—
and have the gall
to ask if I'm wearing lipstick.

What a tactic.

And here I sit
with a pallid smile,
heart thumping with all its might,
and all the while
I debate if I even have the right
to feel this.

Different Worlds

You called it a reality check.
Told me we live in different worlds.

Yes, I'm aware—
you're the kind who books a flight on a whim.
You fly first class, sip champagne.
And I—
I've never even stepped on a plane.
Somehow, that makes me dim?

My life revolves around illness, pain—
and for that, you offer disdain?

No careful words today, no soft tone—
did the Barcelona sun turn you to stone?

Or is it now she'll have you back,
and I refused to crack,
that you can now use my life
to excuse what you lack?

Well—no matter how bright the sun,
no matter what you've become,
you're still council estate scum.

Just like me.
Minus the integrity.

Provocative Statement

"...'Cept the man I wanted
didn't want me."

It was a throwaway line—
just words,
but ferociously mine.

You called it
a provocative statement.

Said you did.
Still do.

But you said that before—
and proved it untrue.

Unchanged

So we find ourselves standing
in this dismal, poky kitchen—
suspended in the poignant lull
that followed your latest recommendation.

Then you repeated,
for my amusement,
that exaggerated, effeminate pose,
drawing from me
the faintest smile—
an adoring headshake.

And in that moment,
I almost forgot.

For that fleeting breath of time,
things felt unchanged.

But as I consider the man before me—
eyes sweeping, slowly down—
my weak smile fades.

Because from greying head
to black-socked foot,
I adore you still.
And I always will.

The Hug

"Can I have a hug?" you ask,
grimacing like you already know
I should say no.

And I should.
But I don't.

I come to you without pause.
My morals shout—
keep it brief.
Keep it platonic.
Keep your distance.

But you,
in that selfish, thoughtless,
or perhaps
telepathic way,
bring us chest to chest.

You shuffle—closer.
A careful inch.
And then another.

And I feel it—
firm against me,
separated only
by cotton and denim.

You don't move.
But neither do I.

My head rests
on the warm weight of your chest,
and I'm too aware—
too deeply aware—

of my breasts
flattened against you,
the cruel gentleness
of you.

That soft, quiet place
I've rested once,
twice—
never enough.

This is going on too long.
You're going too far.
You know this is wrong.

But in my arms
is the man I love—
so just once,
let me be.

Let me have this.

I'm about to pull away—
already retreating—
when you rest your chin on my head.

Hot breath
seeps into my scalp.
And just like that,
my eyes close.

No More

You tried to kiss me
after all that—
after her.

You cruel rat.

I pulled away.

"No.
No more."

Your hands came up—
cautious male surrender.

I saw the resignation.

And in that look,
you dared
to make me
the heartless one.

McCain? Oven Chips

Just as the last piece of my heart broke
I stood and made an awfully witty joke
about McCain oven chips.

It was so good, it made you laugh fully.
But then you fell silent and gazed—dolefully.

And I gazed back, searching your eyes,
somehow hopeful you'd come to realise
everything you'd lost in me.

Flat 6

The blue carpet,
L-shaped sofa,
skylight spilling calm—
it used to feel
enchanted.

I'd hoped
to lose my virginity here.
To make it matter.

But today,
the place is stripped
of its magic.
Austere.

Like I've been
forgotten,
discarded.

At the door,
you offer *Tristram Shandy*—
your copy.

It takes all my strength
to smile
and say,
"No…
you keep it."

Because we both know
I won't be seeing you again.

Shelf

You surmised
I was just scared
of being left
on the shelf.

Funny—
you always looked
for answers
anywhere
but yourself.

The Last Time I Saw You

There was no
sad, parting embrace,
no guilt, no disgrace—
just a casual
"See ya."

But I watched
the back of your head
until I lost you in the crowd,
just in case.

For Now

You went from
"made for each other"
to "friends for life"—
to "for now."

It's not just you.
It's men.

But really—
it's humans.

So transient.
So fickle.
Promises—
they cripple.

Try loyalty.
Try truth.

Try meaning it.
Live up to it.
Fucking commit.

Heavy Stone

Two weeks of nothing.
I thought
you'd let me go.

Then—
a message.
Your favourite, you said,
was *Heavy Stone*.

Was it code?
A clever goodbye?
A trace of guilt
you meant to imply?

I replayed it—
again, again.
Searched each line
thinking it your farewell letter,
a sign.

You'd carried
your cold heart
home.

Absence

I snigger at myself—
the derision is real,
but the hope
still lingers.

That foolish, quiet hope
you'd pull up
outside my garden gate,
to be near.

To pass through
this market town
just to feel
what we were.

I tell myself
it's madness.
But I still glance
at every passing car.

Possible

Is it asking too much—
just for one
single man
to love me
as I am?

I just need to know
one can.

Break Up

You once told me
that a break up
is like a form of grief.

At the time, I scoffed—
but you were right.

Except it's worse—
much worse.

Because unlike in death
there's ever that
useless, wasted belief.

21/58

"If I were thirty years younger,
we'd be kind of made for each other,
wouldn't we?"

That's what you said.

What do you mean *would be*?
I simply was.

And still—
you chose her instead.

Reminders

Yorkshire cricket.
A country thicket.

Leeds United.
Love, unrequited.

Rolled Rs.
Dire Straits' guitars.

Intellectual snarking.
Philip Larkin.

Bob Dylan.
Rooting for the villain.

The Beach Boys.
Background noise.

Beano books.
Toy fire trucks.

Decent thrillers.
Serial killers.

Leonard Cohen.
Wilfred Owen.

York.
Theatrical talk.

Folklore.
TV gore.

All these reminders—
cruel little rewinders.

Words

I hoped
my words might reach you—
say all I couldn't manage to.

That a line
might settle beneath your ribs
and quietly build a shrine.

But with a snort and grin,
you tossed them in the bin.

Almosts

We nearly kissed
by the old brick wall,
by the museum,
on the bench,
in the car.

We're a list of places
where it didn't happen.

And still,
I ache for every one.

Reliance

I know what it is now.
That scent.

It's all of it—
the cling of our homes
hanging in the aisle,
settling into the upholstered seats
hoovered by a dusty old Henry.

Sweet, stale rags
doused in polish.
Metal, plastic, diesel fumes.
The musty scalps
of the elderly in front of me.

The perfume, the fabric softener,
the deodorants, lotions, colognes—
chemicals trailing behind
young and old alike.

Then the window breathes in
sheep, hemlock, horses,
the dampness of spring fields—
a familiar countryside rot
that winds through every turn.

I rest my temple
against hot, rattling glass.
Conscious of coughs,
I can taste their colds—
yet every lungful
is a reverie.

My body still thinks
this journey means you.

Except it doesn't.
And it never will do.

The Market Square

All these years and it only just occurs to me
what's positioned underneath this slate canopy:

at my back, stands an erect stone phallus,
and I can't help but think God is being callous.

I came and perched on these dappled slabs to brood,
'cause I'm in that melancholic kind of mood.

From here, I sit and observe this overpopulated town,
and as ever, it's like the saturation's been turned down.

Everything's just a varying shade of graphite.
I am an alien species who detests everyone in sight.

But the bus pulls in—that vivid green and yellow
hitting me with cruel anticipation, before leaving me hollow.

People pile on—it hisses—and leaves without me
taking those other people—all those *normal people*—to my city.

Left alone to watch the leaves skitter and twirl,
I resist the urge to burst, to weep, to hurl,

as I recall when you parked over there,
how you were once here, in this cobbled square.

Huddled up, cold, on that bench, I heard you call my name.
You've no idea what I'd give to hear your voice again.

And that first day you came, this slab was my seat.
Even thirty yards away, spotting you was such an easy feat—

it wasn't the neon jacket, it was my eyes: they sought you.

They still do.

I remember thinking how no one here, nor elsewhere,
could even begin to compare.

But I look over to Boots, and you're not there.
You're never coming back. There's to be no love affair.

Yet I see you strolling over, sticking out your tongue
and I wish I had hugged you, then—I wish I had clung.

But two years on, and now a quarter-of-a-century old,
I know all that'll ever penetrate me is the cold.

I let it seep into my pelvis, until I'm one with eroding stone—
All the ways I have grown, and all I wish I had shown.

Still

You're a fucking knob.
But the thing is—
just the thought of you
is somehow still enough
to make me
throb.

The Plea

Sketch me a tree.
tell me again of those voyages,
souls lost at sea.

Smirk at me—admiringly.
Gaze at me—silently.
Enlighten and empower me.

It's not so much a request, as a plea:
come back to me.

York

When I was a kid,
York was magic.
It was my Diagon Alley—
cobbled streets,
narrow Snickelways,
old buildings leaning in
like they whispered secrets
beneath the tourist din.

The air thrummed
with folklore.
Invisible,
but so palpable
I swore I'd glimpse
something more
if I stood still long enough—
if I just let it come to me.

I imagined a hellhound
prowling around,
brownies beneath windowsills,
ghouls pressed
to the stone walls—
watchful eyes
enough to give chills.

Then came you.
Now Stonegate whispers
your name—
and everywhere else
feels just the same.

Every corner
a cherished place,

each one
still carrying your trace.

The streets I loved
are monuments—
not to folk tales,
but to old moments.

For two years,
I haven't stepped foot
within the city walls.

The closest I get
is Wiggington Road—
a glimpse of the Minster calls
just before we turn off
for the hospital.

It always catches me—
there,
in the distance.

So close.
Yet so out of reach.

I can't go back.
Not while you still haunt it.
Not while it still feels
like
you.

X O'Clock

It's the one time of day
I know exactly where you are—
exactly what you're drinking,
exactly what you're thinking.

I trace your footsteps
in my head.

You're not lost,
not absent,
not unreachable.

You're not even far.

I could go,
if I wanted.
But I am un—
wanted.

So I sit here,
trapped
in another time.

October

I used to love October—
now I can't wait for it to be over.
But it was my month. Mine.
To moon over folklore,
to plunge into true crime,
to feel Halloween to the core—
but not anymore.

It was the one time of year
the shops would have me cheer,
at home in the morbid aesthetic:
orange, black, and blood red—
most of it tacky, pathetic,
but still, it sat right in my head.
Who could resist a gory bedspread?

I used to relish the autumn eves,
wading through the rusting leaves,
chimney smoke thick in the air.
I'd wonder what a thought could raise,
what might stir out there,
in the longer nights, the shorter days—
perfect for my vampire ways.

But I will confess—
it did always severely depress:
the trick-or-treaters from '*Frozen*',
the Marvel heroes, the slutty nurses;
it's not what I would have chosen.
They don't appreciate curses,
or feel the weight of hearses.

I'd undress by my window,
look for Barghest skulking below.
At 2am, I'd still be awake,

half-watching '*Nosferatu*',
searching for a spooky bake.
But now I don't know what to do—
it's like it's all owned by you.

But as I study David Parker Ray,
you woo with a pumpkin latte.
My pumpkins: carved masterpieces—
but you didn't see such riches
and that tears me into pieces.
I want to think of witches,
not you pulling at britches.

You left me haunted—
left me dead, but daunted.
I feel like I'm possessed.
I used to find peace in the moon,
now it leaves me hollow, at best.
You and I—once so in tune,
living with ghosts, even in June.

Morality Jar

Dear God,
can I interest you in a bargain?

See—
I've been filling my morality jar
with good-deed tokens,
even while walking around
feeling lifeless
and broken.

Tell me—
would I still be forsaken
if I asked
to cash them all in
for just one night
with a man
who's taken?

When Memories Invade the Night

I can't sleep.
You're in my throat,
my chest,
behind my eyelids—
there's no rest.

I've lost entire days
to your solemn gaze.
With your provoking smirk,
you linger,
you lurk.

Three, four times a night
I try to exorcise you—
my own hands,
a conjuring, a rite.

I watch myself
in the mirror's view,
like you might be watching, too.

But there's no release.
And you don't show.
So I curl around the aftershock
and beg for peace
into a damp pillow.

Thud

I only charged my phone
for a dentist appointment.
Hadn't used it
in over a year.

Then her words lit the screen.

Thud.

Cheek to carpet.
No breath.
No scream.
Just
numb.

She said you laughed at me
in bed.

Said it was all
inside my head—

a mere case of pity.

And you—
you let her.

Ad Hominem

This is what I get for bowing out gracefully.
This is my thanks for putting her—
a complete stranger—
before my own desires.

A woman of sixty,
going after my self-esteem
like some bitchy, emotionally-inept teen,
all while boasting of polyamory.

Well—sorry to have been so considerate,
for naively thinking after
over thirty years of marriage
it just might've hurt.

But I'm curious:
if so proudly polyamorous,
why the savage signing off as his "Mrs"
and for what?
In her words— a few "tame" kisses?

You know what I think the problem is?
I think she's actually a little jealous.

And if her words weren't so hurtful,
it would almost be humorous.

Everybody But Me

From young kids yet to hit puberty
to the most decrepit elderly,
from the wall-licking barmy
to those with a debilitating disability,
tall, short, fat or skinny—
even the downright fucking ugly,

and those crows up in the chimney—

it is
literally
everybody

but me.

Maggoty Work

To go ahead and seduce a sensitive first-timer,
who in many ways was still just a minor,

to go to great lengths to earn her trust,
in the pursuit of satisfying your own lust,

to offer to be the one steadfast exception,
after a life of fear, heartache and rejection,

to carefully construct all your sentences,
in the hopes of better improving your chances,

and after all that, to just casually walk away,
just as she'd started to believe you might stay,

to show no concern for her emotions,
but leave her confused and heartbroken,

to go on to shift the blame and tell lies,
and permit wifey to mock, threaten and criticize,

and say nothing, but just lie back and smirk,
that was indeed some maggoty work.

Rare

Oh, the times I've sat and moped over how I compare—
questioned whether they're natural, petite, or fair.
They won't be fat—I certainly know that!
I'll bet they're the sort who take hours to prepare.

The times I've wondered if they have any artistic flair,
if you're ever intrigued by what they have to share.
They won't be ugly—but are they as pretty?
Tell me, in what ways do these new women ensnare?

The times I've laid awake at night in despair,
thinking how my absence didn't in the least bit impair.
But them—they'll soon fuck you, I know that's true.
To them, it's a bit of fun, a rush, they don't care.

But then, neither do you.

The times you mocked me, said I just didn't dare—
yet it was your wife's feelings I was trying to spare.
But for words, I cop blame - I'm ridiculed, branded tame,
and you know what? That is so bloody unfair!

The times I've thought of them, up there in your lair,
how they must writhe and moan and lay bare.
But they can't excite, not nearly as much as I might,
because, despite what you think, I had no damned fright.

And the times I'd have wiped your arse when old, I swear—
I was content to be with you, it didn't matter where.
I'd have loved you, if you had nothing but your mind—
be it sixty or eighty, I'd have still been there.

So all the times they're coming onto you—be aware,
it's not you, but that dreaded status, the mysterious air.

Oh, they can gloat: 'I banged that bloke in the long, black coat!'
but you'll never again find one so loyal, and so rare.

Impulse

Most days, I don't know
whether I want to screw you
or press your face
to the gravel under my shoe.

Usually both.

I want to feel your growth
as you cry out an oath.

I want you to taste
everything you did to me—
hard, brutal, ugly—
and choke on ecstasy.

Fool

Never give consistent tenderness
to a damaged and lonely girl,
because it will mean the world.
It will make such a change
from feeling worthless,
that her instinct will be to
offer her heart in exchange.

But it wasn't that you wanted,
was it?

Six-Stone-Thirteen

I've dropped to six-stone-thirteen.
It wasn't exactly a personal goal—
I'm just lacking
the weight of a soul.
The one you stole.

Mum said I look poorly, like a pre-teen.
Suppose this is how it manifests—
but it's not like
I need my breasts.

I'm a well-disciplined machine,
throwing precision punches
at the hole—
at what could have been—
making sure
I'm too lean,
too resilient and mean,
to ever
lose
control.

The Wolf Spider and I

I have a visitor.

He inches across the exposed floorboards
of the bathroom,
pausing at the strap of my discarded bra,
one leg testing,
then another,
feeling his way along the fabric
like it's betraying everything about me.

He descends into the curve of the cup,
then down into the hollow of my battered,
oily, moccasin slipper.
From there, he peers up.

Facing me.

Something in his movements—
too slow, too deliberate.
He lingers, like he knows.

Until he arrived, I'd been sat
motionless in lukewarm water,
absently staring
at crumbling plaster,
listening to the neighbours'
cheap, thumping music.

It's too loud to think.
and I'm too dull to feel.

But now, the wolf spider
shares the room with me.

He doesn't scurry.
Doesn't flee.
And I don't flinch.

We—
two grotesque,
intolerable things,
sit with one another.

His company was unexpected,
but welcome.

Strangers

They watch you
like you're
something foreboding.

Hang on your words.
Tilt their heads.
Eyes wide.
Open-mouthed.

They leave
amused, impressed—
or none the wiser.

To them,
you're charm.
A performance
worth shivering for.

And I hate them.

Wish, some nights,
that I could see you
as they do—
just for an hour.

Not significant.
Not devastating.
Just unknown
but near.

The Shoebox

All that's left of us
fits inside a shoebox.

A faded bus ticket,
a cinema stub—
Under the Skin.
Half a dozen photos
of you,
but never one
of us
together.

A note I never sent.
Poems I wrote
but couldn't give.

I keep it in the drawer
next to my bed.

But this—
this is what love looks like.

A pitiful archive,
but much-needed proof
of me once feeling alive.

Ashes

Your ghost
lives in that album.
It holds you
like a djinni.

I see your silhouette rise,
curling around
her shrill, haunting cries.

I see your solemn eyes.
Your essence—
it's contained, long-lasting—
in her whispered rasping.

I put it on
to suffer.
To feel.
Like cutting into memory—
a wound I won't let heal.

It's the sacrifice I make
just to keep you real.

Chess

I'm a black chess piece.
I let you move first,
but I play well—
calculated,
always thinking ahead.

But you—
you were neither black nor white.
You arrived as something grey.

And I didn't know
how to move against that.

Three Videos

All that I have left of you now
are three measly videos on my PC.
I can stay up watching them 'til gone 3,
but you don't look at the camera
the way you used to look at me.

Your Name

It's just a word.
But every time I see it—
something sharp,
uninvited,
intimate.

Like the world
accidentally
spoke you aloud.

Summertime

The sunshine spills across the sky,
and once again, I sit and cry.
I'm indoors—miserable, withdrawn,
hair unwashed, the curtains drawn.

I pine for fields where no one sees—
for us, making love among the bees—
your skin still slick with shower heat,
my lips exploring, slow and sweet.

I want to walk through woods in bloom,
to peel away this flaking gloom,
to wear a dress that lifts in breeze,
and laugh at nothing, feel at ease.

But each bright day, I grow colder,
more afraid, more bitter, older.
I feel like a waste of skin—a blight—
best kept away from all human sight.

The Pretend Partaker

I am the pretend partaker,
seated in Caffè Antichrist,
dolefully reminiscing
about how you once enticed.

I am the sour observer,
the lone sipper of
tepid, milky tea—
pitifully pained by sight of an
unassuming mug and saucer.

You are not coming to meet me.

But the warm scent of coffee
makes me disbelieve this,
and I came seeking precisely that—
to taunt myself with old bliss.

Pretty Dresses

I have so many dresses
hanging in my wardrobe—
ones I wanted to hitch up
as I tasted your earlobe.

I'd only just begun
to feel like a woman—
like your tiny, coveted hourglass.
I was only starting to relish
my newfound feminine sass.

I felt your desire for haste
as your eyes drifted to my waist.
I felt the raw female power
of my own body
as I took a shower.

But now, I may as well burn the lot.
Because there's no more you
to want what I've got.

There's no more going into town—
just sitting miserably around
in fluffy socks
and an unwashed dressing gown.

Brown Quilted Coats

I see one,
and it floors me.

The colour,
the cut—
too close
to what you wore.

My body reacts.
It forgets
you're gone.

Top Hats and Canes

I can't see a man
in a top hat or a cane
without it dragging up
a flicker of pain.

The black gloves and coat
make hope catch in my throat.

And I shouldn't feel it—
but God, I do:

I'm aroused by undertakers
because they dress
just like you used to.

September

I saw your leaflets in a shop in Thirsk today.
I was just stood looking at a few keyrings
when I noticed them at the back of the rack.
And thanks to you two, came crushing dismay—
I now think myself sick for having feelings,
feel humiliated for just having seen.

So I placed the keyring back in the wooden tray
and told myself I wasn't entitled to any longing,
that I should leave this place and not come back.
And I knew what everyone in here would say—
I betted anything they'd laugh at my little fling.
To everyone else, it may as well not have been.

But then I thought, *'Fuck what they'd all say—*
I had the courage to express my feelings.
It happened, whether or not it involved cock,
so if people judge me for loving then – hey,
they can go ahead. To me, it meant everything.
And no matter what, my conscience is clean.'

So I picked up a leaflet from the display,
and as expected, the full view sent me reeling –
with his younger face, surrounded by black –
and it hurt like it all happened yesterday.
But for the first time in a year, precious grieving,
no longer fazed by them thinking me green.

Relentless

It's Friday night, twenty-past-nine,
and I'm sat in A&E with Lee—
thinking about when you were mine.
I've got a three-and-a-half-hour wait,
sat next to the brother I hate.

'*I Want You Now*' by Depeche Mode
plays over and over in my right ear.
Somehow, it fits this clinical atmosphere.
My heart's plucked with each strum—
a welcome pain from the default numb.

God, it's uncanny how much I relate.
And thing is, I know you're not far away—
little over a mile or so, I would say.
The proximity makes me so restless...
my desire for you is so painfully relentless.

Bullseye

Well, I have to applaud you—
you hit the bullseye clean.
And I don't mean to glorify,
but now it seems obscene
for any other man to even try.

So—congratulations.
You've ruined men for me—
until the day I die.

Esteem

You didn't just
morph yourself into a dream—
my dream—
only to snatch it away
when things didn't go your way,
you had to take with it
all my fragile self-esteem.

How could anyone be so mean?

Flesh-Covered Skeleton

It's strange, isn't it:
love.

How
someone becomes
vital, like oxygen.

A man.
A body.
Just flesh
stretched over a skeleton.

Contained offal.
Soft parts.
Warm meat.

He coughs,
burps,
farts.
He sits for a shit—
he does all of it.

He picks his nose,
bumps his head;
he forgets
what I said.
He has morning breath,
and he'll age
until death.

He's not perfect.
Not divine.
But somehow,
I still desperately need him
to be mine.

Red Raggedy Jumper

I've still got that red jumper.
I know you won't even care, or remember.
But it was the jumper I wore
that day, when you last held me.

Except now, it's four years later
and raggier than all my others put together—
a threadbare mess, thanks to the odd pet claw.

Truth is, I'll probably still have it
when I turn eighty-four.

I'm Sorry

I'm sorry
for turning you into a statue of gallantry—
it was something you never claimed to be.

I stood you on that pedestal
while our love was still hypothetical.

And I'm sorry
for loving you so quickly,
while being so guarded, so prickly.

But I'm not sorry
for folding my arms
against your charms,
when all I wanted was to be held,
for my fears to be quelled—
for setting you test after test
to see if you were like the rest.

Because you're not at all sorry
that you were yet another man
who got bored and ran.

The One

Give me a bloke who loves animals as much as yours truly,
who gets out on the street, and fights for equality,
who'll defend the life of an ant, a spider, a bee—
no matter how many people scoff or call him a sissy.
Now, that's the kind of chap I'd stand beside proudly.

I don't want some young chav who prefers *'Call of Duty'*,
his iPhone, drugs, clubs, or Tinder to my company.
Keep your unsolicited dick-pics and posy mirror selfie,
six-packs and branded boxers mean nothing to me.
As for stylish 'dos and cologne—they reek of vanity!

But a grown man with manners—someone gentlemanly?
Yes, now you see—that appeals to me greatly.
I'll take a guy who'll dote on me, treat me like a priority,
who'll say and do thoughtful little things, intuitively,
and be ever intrigued by my skills and identity.

Tall or short, skinny or tubby—it doesn't matter to me,
though I do have a thing for blue eyes, no apology.
I say ick to the most coveted man in the room—seriously!
Give me the self-deprecator, secure but humble,
even if he thinks himself average, old, or ugly.

I prefer a man with a face full of character to study,
who dresses for comfort, not street credibility.
And you know what else I think is super sexy?
A man who'll dance in the street, sober, no matter how badly,
or dress in drag without fear of losing masculinity.

In truth, I'd like a teetotaller—or as near as one can be—
who, like me, can still be the life of any party.
Spare me the louts who mock and ridicule me
for saying I don't drink, nor need it to be worldly,

or to be fun, lively, or bolder than he.

I need a soul I can look to for unwavering stability—
a man who feels honoured to be my sanctuary,
whose wisdom can console all my morbidity,
proud to be what's left of my faith in humanity,
when my heart's blackened by Man's misery.

I want someone who's just as antisocial as me,
another loner, dark, and world-weary,
often content in his own, contemplative company,
a little bit haunted, yet finds peace next to me,
where we can both just quietly be.

I want a lover who'll make love both softly and passionately,
without ever thinking he's somehow conquering me,
but instead prefers to submit, and bring me ecstasy.
He'll communicate openly, earnestly,
at ease to express himself with vulnerability.

I want to be kissed gently, deeply – longingly,
looked upon adoringly, with a love that's easy.
I want to never have to question his loyalty,
and his presence will bring a beauty to all I see,
and draw out the brightest side of me.

The man I wait for is one who can out-sleep me,
yet stay up discussing a book, a film, a documentary,
and ponder the wonders of Earth from the settee—
a man with things to share, and a mind to teach me,
but never feel the need to speak condescendingly.

Judge as you will—I'll wait forever if needs be—
for someone who shares in my integrity,
who values a love that grows patiently,

and finds happiness in the simplest of things,
content just to walk through life with me.

III

The First

First time back on a bus
in five years.
Still hurt.
York still carried us
in the pavement.

But I went—for the animals.

Life had no meaning.
I'd given up
on ever feeling whole—
I was resigned to living
with this gaping hole.

I got on with the task,
put on my Guy Fawkes mask,
held up a 'Truth' sign
and felt a flicker of purpose
I couldn't yet define.

Then he wandered into view—
blue jeans,
even bluer eyes,
white hair,
a mischievous, boyish air.

He teased the little leaflet girl,
asked why she didn't give one
to the Chinese couple.

She giggled—
"'Cause I don't speak Chinese!"

He, mock-outraged, said—
"What do you mean
you don't speak Chinese—
at your age?"

She laughed.
And so did I.

Same humour.
Same accent.
I lament.

A pang of dread—
my heart,
it turns out,
wasn't dead.

Inside Number 9

You recommended it.
Of course you did.
It's like you always knew
who I'd grow into.

As it happens,
I never watched it.
But one day, my husband,
he sat me down
after we'd been out in town,
insisted on the episode
with the concrete bath
and the insects.

He knew, too.

It's now my favourite thing.
And when we watched the final episode
I felt a little sting.

That's ten years
since you and me.

Sometimes
it's a little eerie
how alike you are.

But if nothing else
it proves

I almost
got it right.

Acknowledgements

To mama, first and foremost, for always believing in me, most especially when I didn't believe in myself, and for always encouraging me to keep writing. To my Burton, for giving me the safest place to look back from—your peaceful, steady love made finishing this collection possible. And to Astra, my wonderful editor—thank you for your guidance, your belief, and the long hours you gave to this book. I couldn't have done it without any of you.

www.ingramcontent.com/pod-product-compliance
Lightning Source LLC
Chambersburg PA
CBHW020341010526
44119CB00048B/550